YOUR KNOWLEDGE HAS VALUE

- We will publish your bachelor's and master's thesis, essays and papers

- Your own eBook and book - sold worldwide in all relevant shops

- Earn money with each sale

Upload your text at www.GRIN.com
and publish for free

Bibliographic information published by the German National Library:

The German National Library lists this publication in the National Bibliography; detailed bibliographic data are available on the Internet at http://dnb.dnb.de .

Imprint:

Copyright © 2014 GRIN Verlag, Open Publishing GmbH
Print and binding: Books on Demand GmbH, Norderstedt Germany
ISBN: 9783668295674

This book at GRIN:

http://www.grin.com/en/e-book/339740/african-american-vernacular-english-and-its-use-in-their-eyes-were-watching

Leonie Weißweiler

Aus der Reihe: e-fellows.net stipendiaten-wissen

e-fellows.net (Hrsg.)

Band 2115

African American Vernacular English and its Use in "Their Eyes Were Watching God" by Zora Neale Hurston

GRIN Publishing

GRIN - Your knowledge has value

Since its foundation in 1998, GRIN has specialized in publishing academic texts by students, college teachers and other academics as e-book and printed book. The website www.grin.com is an ideal platform for presenting term papers, final papers, scientific essays, dissertations and specialist books.

Visit us on the internet:

http://www.grin.com/

http://www.facebook.com/grincom

http://www.twitter.com/grin_com

Contents

1 AAVE in public consciousness

African American English (AAVE) was first brought to the attention of linguists when in the 1960s, the government realised that African American (AA) children from urban ghettoes were worse in school than white pupils. To counteract this, it financed compensation programmes in which AA children should be taught Standard English (SE) "by means of structural drills and techniques adopted from foreign language learning" (Schneider 1989: 12, as cited in [Kau02]). When this approach failed, linguists suggested that AA children only spoke a different dialect than white children and that consequently, it would be necessary to teach them SE as an additional dialect. However, this approach also failed because the failure of AA children in school seems to be a result of a cultural and social divide between AA and white American society, of which separate dialects of English are only a symptom [Kau02].

Then in 1978, the Oakland, California, School Board passed a resolution recognizing AAVE (or as they termed it, Ebonics, on the use of this expression see 2.2) as a language and instructing its schools to "devise and implement the best possible academic program for imparting instruction to African American students in their primary language for the combined purposes of maintaining the legitimacy and richness [...]and to facilitate their acquisition and mastery of English language skills" [ORE] It further decreed that the funding for the implementation of this resolution were to be provided by the State. This decision initiated a big public debate about the legitimacy of 'Ebonics' and AA culture in general, which was further fuelled by the Ann Arbor case in 1979, also known as the 'Black English trial'. Eleven AAs had been "placed in remedial speech education classes based in pathological linguistics evaluations which failed to take into account their linguistic heritage as speakers of [...] AAVE" [MRB98](282). Judge Joiner ruled that "the students were using a systematic variety [and] that a barrier of learning resulted when the school did not take into account the children's use of language" [Gre02](222). However supportive of the recognition and emancipation of AAVE as language these decisions were, they were strongly criticised by the public and the old prejudice that AAVE is just AAVE is just English with mistakes is still largely spread.

It will therefore be the aims of this paper to prove this belief wrong and prove that AAVE is indeed a rule-governed language, to investigate its origins and its use in Zora Neale Hurston's most famous novel, Their Eyes Were Watching God.

2

2 Definition of AAVE

2.1 Definition

African American Vernacular English is an ethnic and social dialect spoken by African Americans who are members of the socioeconomically lower class [Gre02](5f.) and Schneider 1989: 5 as cited in [Kau02] (11). However, this dialect is by no means spoken by all African Americans.

2.2 A note on terms

Over the course of the (albeit rather short) history of the public awareness and later, scientific study, of AAVE, a large number of labels have been given for this variety of English. A list is given below:

- Negro dialect
- Nonstandard Negro English
- Negro English
- American Negro English
- Black communications
- Black Dialect
- Black folk speech
- Black street Speech
- Black English
- Black vernacular English
- Afro American English
- African American English
- African American Language
- **African American Vernacular English**

[Gre02]

The creation and use of these labels is of course not arbitrary. Negro and Black were used accordingly to the labels for African Americans at the time.

Additionally "'English' is included in a number of the labels for AAE, which suggests that some of its characteristics are common to or very similar to those of different varieties of English. Along these same lines, 'English' has been omitted from some of these labels in an effort to highlight African and creole relations" [Gre02](6).

Of these labels, African American English, African American Vernacular English and Ebonics are the ones most commonly used today. "In recent publications, AAVE and AAE seem to be used interchangeably, the former probably stressing the working-class setting, the latter emphasizing that it is not a straightforward task to identify the vernacular exactly. [...] These terms are almost entirely academic ones. Most African Americans would possibly name their speech 'Black English' or [...] 'Ebonics'." [Kau02](11). Ebonics is a term coined by the press (Ebony + phonics) and is not used in scientific discussion of the subject, therefore it does not appear in the above list.

In this paper, I have decided to use 'African American Vernacular English' as all the situations where it is used in Hurston's novel are in an informal, working-class setting and I will in chapter 6.2 further investigate the intentions behind and challenges of putting vernacular language into print.

3 Theories about the origins of AAVE

There is a long standing debate among linguists about the origins of AAVE. Traditionally, there are two different camps: the dialectologists and the creolists. The dialect hypothesis claims that "the grammatical core of contemporary AAVE developed from an English base, many of whose features have since disappeared from all but a select few varieties [...], whose particular sociohistorical environment have enabled them to retain reflexes of features no longer attested in Standard English. [Thus] many grammatical distinctions between contemporary varieties of AAVE and American and British English are relatively recent developments" (Poplack 2000:1 as cited in [Kau02]: 5). In opposition, the creolists hold that AAVE started as a creole[1] similar the creoles spoken in the Caribbean as "creole speech might have been introduced to the American colonies through the large number of slaves imported from the colonies of Jamaica and Barbados, where creoles were common" (Rickford 1999b: 327, as cited in [Kau02] (5). This theory is also called the

---

[1]'creole' here meaning a pidgin language that has become the native language of a new generation

substrate hypothesis because "it is argued that the West African or substrate languages influenced the sentence and sound structures of AAE" [Gre02](9).

However, it is of course highly difficult to find reliable sources for the reconstruction of both AAVE and the southern white vernacular as a vernacular is rarely used in print and even if it were, the AA slaves of that time did not have the means to write down or print anything that would have endured until the present. Almost the same circumstances hold true for the southern white vernacular and for English creoles. The study and comparison of these is naturally the only basis for the investigation of the origins of AAVE [Kau02](5).

Kautzsch ([Kau02]: 4-6) opts for a compromise: he thinks that "this dichotomy is not a categorical one. The dialectologists have never 'excluded the possibility of a previous creole stage of Black English, expecially with respect to the initial stages of slavery, nor have they denied the existence of African or creole remnants in the present-day dialect' (Schneider 1989: 25). On the contrary, most creolists concede that some influence of white speech on black 'is clearly to be expected, but the degree and importance of this influence is thought to be relatively limited' (Schneider 1989: 25)." He then suggests that "an integrative approach that takes into account both sides is most likely to deliver the mot [sic] accurate assessment of the status and the evolution of AAE" [Kau02](6). Similarly, Winford (1997) goes for a "compromise between the traditional creolists view and the more moderate dialectologist view" [Win97](307) and gives three explanations for the development of the features of AAVE: 1) several features from earlier varieties of English were adopted into AAVE, 2) many features appear to have resulted from imperfect second language learning and 3) several features can be explained as a result of retention of creole structure and meaning [Win97].

4 A Comparison of AAVE and SE

4.1 Syntax

4.2 General Remarks

When examining the syntactic features of AAVE, it is important to realise that none of the properties of AAVE are unique. As Mufwene et al. (1998: 119) argue, "AAVE is generally not unique: those syntactic structures purportedly found only in AAVE are in fact part of the dialects spoken by other groups, especially but not limited to Anglo-American vernacular English speakers who live in the southern United States". [MRB98]

4.2.1 Obvious and camouflaged differences

In order to describe the Syntax of AAVE and to prove that it is a systematic variety, it is important to first understand that some of the most obvious differences "do not involve differences in syntax but rather the lexical peculiarities of certain AAVE verbs." (Mufwene et al. 1998: 12). They are thus irrelevant for the underlying structure of AAVE. Examples are the use of *go* to denote the static location of an object or an intransitive form of the verb *beat*. In contrast, there are "AAVE structures which at first look similar or identical to those in other varieties of English, but which in fact mask underlying differences" [MRB98](13). This is called linguistic camouflaging: "the phenomenon in which a vernacular form closely resembles a standard form while being different in structure or meaning" [MRB98](14). Examples for this are the aspectual marker *be* (see chapter 4.1.8) and the tell-say-construction (see chapter 4.1.11).

4.2.2 Negative concord

Negative concord, or multiple negation, is "the use of two or more negative morphemes to communicate a single negation" [MRB98](17) when in SE, a sentence must not contain more than one negative morpheme. However, this does not automatically mean that all negatable forms in that sentence have to be negated.

a) Ain't nobody gonna spend no time going to no doctor.

b) Nobody is going to spend any time going to a doctor.

Where AAVE in a) permits more than one negative morpheme in one sentence, SE uses at least on negative polarity item (NPI); "a quantifier word or phrase(e.g. any, ever, a bit) that occurs within the 'scope' of the negative" [MRB98](18). Negative concord in AAVE should not be confused with logical double negation found in most other dialects. In that case, one negative morpheme undoes the other to form an emphatic positive. Logical double negation sentences can – in speech – be distinguished from negative concord sentences by the stress usually laid on one of the two negative morphemes [MRB98](17-18).

6

4.2.3 Negative inversion

Negative inversion sentences are sentences in which subject and auxiliary change places (subject-auxiliary-inversion, [MRB98](26). These sentences occur with "supporting do [...], aspectual [...] or linking be [...] or a modal" [MRB98](26) in existential sentences. While most linguists argue that negative inversion is used to place additional emphasis on the negation, Green ([Gre02]: 80) disagrees and states that "a number of factors in addition to the initial placement of the negated auxiliary can determine prominence".

4.2.4 Question formation

The most apparent difference in AAVE and SE question formation is the possibility of a non-inverted question in the former. A non-inverted question is a "direct question without inversion of the subject and auxiliary verb, usually with rising intonation" ([Ric99]: 8). Non-inversion is only possible when the subject is represented by a relatively short noun phrase. Although not a feature unique to AAVE, this kind of question formation is not found in other varieties of English [MRB98](29).

4.2.5 Tense

The tenses of AAVE are given in the following. Other phenomena like the omission of the copula or any phonological variation are ignored for the moment in the example sentences.

- **Present tense, e.g. "I/he eat"**
- Past tense, e.g. "I/he ate"
- **Preterite *had*, e.g. "I/he had ate"**
- Future tense, e.g. "I/he will eat"
- **Present progressive, e.g. "I'm eating"/"He eating"**
- Past progressive, e.g. "I/he was eating"
- Future progressive, e.g. "I/he will be eating"
- **Present perfect, e.g. "I/he ate"**
- **Past perfect, e.g. "I/he had ate"**

7

- **Present perfect progressive, e.g. "I/he been eating"**

- Past perfect progressive, e.g. "I/he had been eating"

- Modal perfect, e.g. "I/he should have been eating"

The tenses in which the formation differs from that in SE are highlighted in bold print. The following patterns can be found in them:

- "The first person form of the verb may be used with all persons" (Mufwene et al 1998: 42)

- The copula be may be omitted (see 44.1.11)

- The past form (in this example, ate) is also used in present perfect and past perfect in addition to the simple past

- Preterite *had* is an auxiliary to indicate preterite meaning and not the pluperfect

[MRB98](40-42) and [Gre02](36-38)

4.2.6   Aspect

- Habitual, e.g. "I be eating" (I am usually eating)

- Remote past a), e.g. "I been eating" (I have been eating for a long time)

- Remote past b), e.g. "I been ate" (I ate a long time ago)

- Remote past perfect, e.g. "I had been ate" (I had eaten a longtime ago)

- Resultant state, e.g. "I done ate" (I have already eaten)

- Past perfect resultant state, e.g. "I had done ate" (I had already eaten)

- Modal resultant state, e.g. "I should have done ate" (I should have already eaten"

- Remote past resultant state, e.g. "I done ate" (I finished eating a long time ago)

- Remote past perfect resultant state, e.g. "I had been done ate" (I had already eaten a long time ago)

- Habitual resultant state, e.g. "I be done ate" (I have usually already eaten)

- Future resultant state, e.g. I will be done ate" (I will have already eaten)

- Modal resultant state, e.g. "I might be done ate" (I might have already eaten)

  The patterns that can be found in the above aspects are the following:

- Aspectual be "signals the recurrence of a process or state of affairs" (Mufwene 1998: 45)

- Been (or bin, to emphasise the different stress) indicates that the starting point of the action lies in the remote past

- Done denotes the perfective aspect

[MRB98](44-45) and [Gre02](45-47)

4.2.7 Structure of the noun phrase

While most of the formation of the noun phrase resembles that in SE, there are a few significant differences. The associative plural strategy, e.g. "Felicia and them done gone" instead of "Felicia and her friends/family/associates have gone" is a feature that AAVE shares with English creoles rather than with other dialects of English and may be reduced to *nem*, e.g. "Felicia nem done gone". However, this is a phonological feature, not a syntactical one.

In the formation of relative clauses, Mufwene et al. (1998: 76-77) identify the following noteworthy differences:

- The relative pronouns who, which and especially whose are typically not used

- Relative clauses are typically introduced by the null complementizer, by the complementizer that, sometimes by what, which also behaves more like a complementizer than a relative pronoun

- The null complementizer is allowed even when the relative NP is a subject

The absence of the plural marker on the head noun might be mistaken for a syntactical feature, but is explained in terms of a phonological deletion

[MRB98](70-77).

4.2.8 Omission of the copula

The copula *be* may in some cases be omitted. The governing rules of this omission are still subject to debate, however it is relatively clear that the full forms *be* and *was* and the first person singular *am* (or *'m*) may not be omitted. Consequently, the possibility of copula omission applies only to *is* and *are*. [Ric99](62)

4.2.9 The tell-say-construction

The serial verb construction *tell say* marks the beginning of a quotation as in "They tell him say, 'You better not go there'". It can alternate with simple quotative say: "They tell him say, 'You better not go there' say 'It's dangerous'". This is a distinctive feature of AAVE because a comparable serial verb construction cannot be found in other varieties of English [MRB98](13-14).

4.2.10 Double modals

AAVE is one of the dialects of English that can use more than one modal auxiliary in a clause, e.g. "He might could do the work". A number of combinations are possible, occasionally even triple modals, but there are lexical restrictions on which modal verbs can be combined. Bothe modals may be in the same tense or tenses can be mixed, however tense matching is the preferred pattern [MRB98](32-33).

4.3 Phonology

The following provides a by no means exhaustive list of the phonological features of AAVE. It has often been suggested that these arise from the different shape of an AA head or from a 'lazy tongue'. However, this has proven not to be the case.

- Reduction of word-final consonant clusters, especially those ending in [t] or [d]

- Deletion of word-final single consonant (especially nasals) after a vowel

10

- Devoicing of word-final voiced stops after a vowel. The devoiced consonant may be followed or replaced by a glottal stop.

- Realisation of final [] as [n] in gerunds

- Realisation of [θ] as [t] or [f]

- Realisation of [δ] as [d] or [v]

- Realization of *thr* sequences as *th*, especially before [o] and [u]

- Deletion or vocalisation of [l] after a vowel, may have the effect of deleting the "ll" of contracted will

- Deletion or vocalisation of [r] after a vowel. This rule applies more often when the [r] comes at the end of a word and is followed by a word beginning with a consonant rather than a word beginning with a vowel, but it can also apply when a vowel follows within the same word. Grammatical effects may include the use of *they* for the SE possessive *their*.

- Deletion of initial [d] and [g] in certain tense-aspect auxiliaries, the distinctive use of *ain't* for *didn't* probably derives historically from this rule too

- Deletion of unstressed initial and medial syllables

- Metathesis or transposition of adjacent consonants, as in *aks* instead of *ask* (often referred to by the public in the course of the discussion about AAVE, see chapter 1)

- Realisation of [v] and [z] as [b] and [d] respectively, sepecially in word-medial position before a nasal

- Realisation of syllable-initial *str* as *skr*, especially before high front vowels like [i]

- Monophtongal pronunciations of *ay* and *oy*

- Neutralisation/merger of [I] and [ε] before nasals

- Realisation of *ing* as *ang* and *ink* as *ank* in some words

- Stress on first rather than second syllable

- More varied intonation, with higher pitch range and more rising and level final contours than other American English varieties

[Ric99](4-5) and [Gre02](106-133)

4.4 Lexicon

Even without even attempting to give a complete list of all the differences of the AAVE and SE lexicons, there are a few things to be said about the structure of the AAVE lexicon, its usage and its relationship with the SE lexicon. The main differences of these two lexicons can be divided into three parts: words which are exclusive to AAVE, words that are shared by SE but have a different meaning in AAVE and words which are shared by AAVE and SE. AAVE-exclusive words are the main focus of the study of the AAVE lexicon mainly because they are the most obvious difference to SE and are often used to identify an AAVE speaker; as Rickford and Rickford state, "one of the many fascinating features of black vocabulary is how sharply it can divide blacks and whites, and how solidly it can connect blacks from different social classes "(Rickford and Rickford 2000: 93 as cited in [Gre02]: 13); but they also represent a point of interest to those studying the origins of AAVE as some of these words are clearly related to African or creole words. Words with different meanings in AAVE are interesting as an example of linguistics camouflaging (see chapter 4.1.2) and are therefore not among the most prominent features. It also has to be noted that Green ([Gre02]: 13) further divides the AA lexicon into "words and phrases used by members of all age groups and those more likely to be identified with members of a certain age group". 'Slang' terms are of course part of the latter group and not to be confused with those universally used in AAVE. Furthermore, it has to be remarked that AAVE speakers are to an extent which is still the subject of debate capable of code-switching, but are not necessarily from youth able to do this (see chapter 1). Also, the usage of words or phrases does not automatically classify someone as an AAVE speaker, however being an AAVE speaker requires knowledge of its lexicon [Gre02](13).

5 Social implications of AAVE

5.1 Reasons for the ongoing existence of a separate AA dialect

While the origins of AAVE have been discussed in chapter 3, the reasons for its ongoing existence are even more complex. Rickford ([Ric99]: 257) identifies to main factors for determining the reasons for linguistic divergence: ecological and ethological factors. If one considers only the ecological factors, those "having to do with the nature of the contact" [Ric99](257), one would expect AAVE and SE to have converged sooner or later due to the increase of contact that the abolishment of slavery and much later, mass media brought about. As this was clearly not the case, the ethological factors ("emotional and attitudinal factors" ([Ric99](257)) have to be considered. AAVE is, and was, a major factor of identification for AA. It also is, and was, a target of discrimination as "the majority of English speakers think that AAVE is just English with two added factors: some special slang terms and a lot of grammatical mistakes"(Pullum 1999 as cited in [Gre02]: 221) but there also is a consensus between AAs and whites about "the way Whites should speak and the way Blacks should speak" [Ric99](257). These two factors together seem to be able to account for the existence of a separate AA dialect.

5.2   Reasons for the further divergence of AAVE and SE

In the last few decades there has been increasing evidence of a further divergence of AAVE and SE [Kau02](8). This can be attributed to two main factors: an increase of identification with AA culture and apparently ongoing inequalities in American society. Rickford [Ric99] (274) explains the former with different attitudes about AAVE in different generations of AAs: "Black teenagers are less assimilationist than their parents and especially their grandparents, and more assertive about their rights to talk and act in their "natural" way". It seems that the overall attitude of AAs about their culture has changed from trying more or less to "act White" to being proud of their identity (this is of course greatly generalised) (Cf. Rickford 1999d: xiii as cited in [Kau02]: 8). This is another consequence of the second factor: ongoing inequalities in American society. The linguistic discovery of the further divergence of AAVE and SE has some grave social consequences: it indicates that "the segregation of the ethnic groups in the US is still great, although attempts have been made to integrate black people into mainstream US society" [Kau02](8). Apparently this segregation is not only strong enough to prevent large-scale socialising between AAs and Whites, but also enough for many AAs to feel that they are being discriminated against so much that the trend is going towards intentional and voluntary separation.

6 Use in *Their Eyes Were Watching God*

6.1 Zora Neale Hurston's take on AAVE

In her paper The Characteristics of Negro Expression" [?] Zora Neale Hurston attempts to find universal qualities which explain every single feature of African American language and culture. The characteristics that she identifies give a unique insight into her thoughts about AAVE and consequently into her portrayal of AAVE in Their Eyes Were Watching God. The first of these characteristics is drama. Hurston believes that "every phase of Negro life is highly dramatised. [. . .]Everything is acted out. Unconsciously for the most part of course." [?] She then extends this to language and states that "The primitive man exchanges descriptive words. His terms are all close fitting. Frequently the Negro, even with detached words in his vocabulary—not evolved in him but transplanted on his tongue by contact—must add action to it to make it do. [. . .]So we can say the white man thinks in a written language and the Negro thinks in hieroglyphics." [?] She uses this principle of drama and the, according to Hurston, second most important feature, the will to adorn, to explain what she holds to be "the Negro's greatest contribution to the language" [?]: the use of metaphor, simile, the double descriptive and verbal nouns.

While Hurston's effort to take pride in and promote AA culture is certainly commendable, her grasp of it does not go beyond that of a white racist outsider as her strategy for the emancipation is to take white racist prejudices about AA culture and try to convert them into good things. These converted prejudices seem to be the only features of AA culture that she is able to identify. For example, she identifies the white prejudice that AA culture is "lacking in originality" [?]. Rather than challenge this or instead argue that no culture is ever new and that it is human nature to take the present culture and re-interpret it, Hurston instead claims mimicry solely for "the Negro" [?] and elevates it beyond the insults of racists Whites by defining it as "an art in itself" [?]. In principle, however, her grasp of AA culture is the same as that of the white racist outsider. This of course greatly affects her use of AAVE in TEWWG and gives an insight into her intentions in using which I will explore in Chapter 6.2.

6.2 The use of AAVE in Their Eyes

As Hurston was one of the principal writers of the Harlem Renaissance's literary movement, her intention in using AAVE is relatively clear: TEWWG, as her overall work, is driven by a wish to emancipate and represent AA society at the time. Although there was some discussion among the writers of the Harlem renaissance about the suitability of AAVE for literature, Hurston believed AAVE "fully capable of functioning as a literary language and sought to substantiate this belief in their fictional texts" [Boe99](23).

There is no agreement between linguists as to whether Hurston's portrayal of AAVE is authentic, but the better question may be whether Hurston even intended it to be a complete and linguistically accurate representation as her aim may instead have been to "stylise vernacular language for most effective resonance in a written medium" [Boe99](19) and leave the reader to fill in the rest, in accord with the call-and-response tradition in AA culture which she herself identified in "The Characteristics of Negro Expression" [Boe99]. Even if this is not the case, she certainly never intended a portrayal of "universal" AAVE, but of its Florida regional variety [Boe99](19-22, 85-86).

Hurston uses AAVE not only in all the direct speech, but also in some narrative passages:

"It was part of him, so it was alright. She rather found herself angry at imaginary people who might try to criticize. Let the old hypocrites learn to mind their own business and leave other folks alone. Tea Cake wasn't doing a bit more harm trying to win hisself a bit little money than they was always doing with their lying tongues. Tea Cake had more good nature under his toe-nails than they had in their so-called Christian hearts. She better not hear none of them old backbiters talking bout her husband! Please, Jesus, don't let them nasty niggers hurt her boy. " [?](168)

This is the kind of exception that proves the rule: as the passages slowly slips into an inner monologue in the form of direct speech, the language slips into AAVE patterns, thus, she really only uses AAVE for direct speech, whether it is marked as such or not.

References

[Boe99]   Eva Boesenberg. Gender- voice- vernacular. the formation of fe-
          male subjectivity in zora neale hurston, toni morrison and alice
          walker. In *American Studies - A Monograph Series*, volume 77,
          page 23. 1999.

[Gre02]   Lisa J. Green. *African American English. A linguistic introduction.*
          New York, 2002.

[Hur34]   Zora   Neale   Hurston.   The   characteristics   of   ne-
          gro   expression.   http://americainclass.org/wp-
          content/uploads/2012/07/NegroExpression.pdf, 1934.

[Hur13]   Zora Neale Hurston. *Their Eyes Were Watching God.* London, 27
          edition, 2013.

[Kau02]   Alexander Kautzsch. The historical evolution of earlier african
          american english. an empirical comparison of early sources. *Topics
          in English Linguistics*, 38, 2002.

[MRB98]   Salikkoko Mufwene, John Rickford, and Guy Bailey. *African-
          American English. Structure, history and use.* London, 1998.

[ORE]

[Ric99]   John R. Rickford. *African American Vernacular English.* Oxford,
          1999.

[Win97]   Donald Winford. On the origins of african american english. a
          creolist perspective part i: the sociohistroical background. *Di-
          achronica*, 14:305–344, 1997.

YOUR KNOWLEDGE HAS VALUE